Kimchi Recipes

Simple Kimchi Recipes for Newbies

BY

Rachael Rayner

Copyright 2019 Rachael Rayner

License Notes

No part of this Book can be reproduced in any form or by any means including print, electronic, scanning or photocopying unless prior permission is granted by the author.

All ideas, suggestions and guidelines mentioned here are written for informative purposes. While the author has taken every possible step to ensure accuracy, all readers are advised to follow information at their own risk. The author cannot be held responsible for personal and/or commercial damages in case of misinterpreting and misunderstanding any part of this Book

Table of Contents

Introduction 6

   Quick Kimchi 8

   Tropical Flavored Cabbage Kimchi 11

   Kimchi fried rice 14

   Shrimp and Kimchi Rice Bowl 17

   Simple Instant Kimchi Salad 20

   Red Cabbage Kimchi 22

   Kale Chickpea Kimchi Salad 24

   Asian Pears Kimchi 26

   Mushroom Kimchi Fried Rice 28

   Garlic Chives Kimchi 31

   Kimchi Tofu Chicken Soup 33

   Squash Kale Cabbage Kimchi Salad 35

   Scallion Apple Kimchi 37

Pineapple Kimchi 39

Stuffed Onion Kimchi 41

Stuffed Jalapeno Pepper Kimchi 43

Carrot Kimchi 46

Spring Onion Kimchi 49

Pineapple Mango Cucumber Kimchi 51

Mango Kimchi 53

Stuffed Cucumber Kimchi 55

Broccoli Tempeh Kimchi Fried Rice 57

Kale Kimchi 59

Cabbage Radish Pear Kimchi 61

Broccoli Kimchi 63

Spicy Cucumber Onion Kimchi Salad 65

Peach Kimchi 67

Chicken Cabbage Kimchi Stir Fry 69

Kimchi Noodles 71

Watermelon Rind Kimchi 74

Conclusion 76

Author's Afterthoughts 77

About the Author... 78

Introduction

Kimchi is a traditional Korean way of fermenting food and keeping it edible for a long time. But in 2019, the entire world knows about kimchi and its health benefits. Kimchi allows people who do not like vegetables too much to add veggies in their everyday meal. The taste of it is so tangy and spicy that it adds more flavor to your regular dishes. Adding 1-2 spoonful of kimchi to your everyday food makes your food much more interesting and delicious.

People are becoming more interested about kimchi because it has many health benefits too. It is a very good way to preserve food. Sometimes when you buy a bulk of veggies and fruits, you can easily invest some of it to make kimchi.

The book contains traditional Cabbage kimchi, and some unique kimchi recipes like watermelon rind kimchi, and stuffed onion kimchi etc. The book even contains fried rice recipes you can make using kimchi. Chinese fried rice dish gets a Korean twist when you add the spicy Kimchi to it. The book also has few delicious kimchi salad recipes.

Try all the recipes and see which ones you like the most. The variety of the book would cater to people of different appetite.

Quick Kimchi

As the name mentions, it is a quick kimchi recipe that is proved to be super tasty. You do not have to wait for long hours to devour it.

Servings: 1 jar

Total Time: Overnight

Ingredients:

- 2 tbsp chili paste
- 1 Chinese cabbage
- 2 carrots, grated
- 2 tbsp fish sauce
- 3 garlic cloves, crushed
- 1 tbsp brown sugar
- 1 tbsp salt
- 1 inch ginger root, grated
- 3 tbsp rice vinegar

Instructions:

Cut the Chinese cabbage into semi long strips.

Add them to a bowl. Add salt to it and crush using your hands.

Let it sit for about 1 hour.

In a blender, add the ginger, brown sugar, garlic, vinegar, chili paste, and fish sauce. Blend into a smooth paste.

Wash the cabbage with cold water properly.

Add the carrot, add the ginger paste. Mix thoroughly and put into a jar.

Cover with lid and let it ferment overnight.

Put it in the refrigerator. It will be fine for 14 days in the fridge.

Tropical Flavored Cabbage Kimchi

Asian dish is not fulfilled without a tangy and spicy kimchi dish. It uplifts any menu by 10 percent.

Servings: 1 jar

Total Time: 2 days

Ingredients:

- 1 head napa cabbage
- 1 Tbsp sea salt

Fish Sauce

- 2 Tbsp tamari
- 2 Tbsp coconut sugar
- 1/4 cup pineapple juice
- 1/4 cup warm water

Sauce

- 3 Tbsp fresh ginger, diced
- 1 head garlic, diced
- 1 small white onion, diced
- 1/2 cup chili flakes

Instructions:

Combine the sauce ingredients together. Mix well.

Combine the fish sauce mixture together.

Cut the head cabbage in half.

Rub the salt well into the cabbage and let it sit for 1 hour.

Wash the cabbage properly and rinse off the water.

Add the sauce mixture and fish sauce mixture.

Put them into a mason jar. Cover with lid.

Let it ferment for 48 hours or longer.

It will be fine for 1 month in the fridge.

Kimchi fried rice

Fried rice is something Asian loves. When you add kimchi in it, it becomes irresistible.

Servings: 1

Total Time: 20 minutes

Ingredients:

- 1 cup rice
- 1 inch ginger, grated
- ½ cup broccoli, chopped
- 2 carrot cut into strips
- 2 eggs
- 1 lime cut into wedges
- 1 lime juice
- 1 garlic clove, sliced
- 1/3 cup kimchi
- 1½ tbsp rapeseed oil
- 1/3 cup spring onion, sliced

Instructions:

Soak the rice for 10 minutes.

In a pot add 2 cups of water and 1 pinch of salt. Bring it to boil.

Add the rice and cook until it is perfectly cooked. Drain and rinse well.

In a pan heat the oil. Scramble the eggs for 1 minute.

Add the spring onion, garlic, carrots, broccoli, lime juice, ginger and toss for 5 minutes.

Add the kimchi and toss for 3 minutes.

Finally add the rice and toss for 5 minutes.

Serve hot with lemon wedges on top.

Shrimp and Kimchi Rice Bowl

Seafood and rice bowl go really well together. They serve as a great brunch or even dinner. Add your favorite type of kimchi to make the dish even better.

Servings: 2

Total Time: 30 minutes

Ingredients:

- 1 lb. shrimp
- 2 cups mixed vegetables
- 1 cup sushi rice
- 1 cup kimchi
- ¼ purple cabbage, sliced
- 1 tablespoon chili-garlic sauce
- 2 tablespoons peanut oil
- 1 tablespoon brown sugar
- 1 teaspoon sesame seeds
- ¾ teaspoon sea salt
- 3 green onions, sliced

Instructions:

Peel the shrimp and devein them.

Boil the sushi rice until well cooked.

In a large wok, heat the oil.

Fry the green onions for 1 minute.

Add the mixed vegetables, brown sugar, salt and purple cabbage.

Toss for 5 minutes. Add the kimchi and cook for 5 minutes.

Add the chili garlic sauce, sesame seeds and shrimp.

Cook for another 5 minutes.

Finally add the cooked rice and toss for 2 minutes.

Serve hot.

Simple Instant Kimchi Salad

When you do not want to wait for 24 hours for a kimchi, make this instant kimchi salad. It is not the traditional one, but it will give you the glimpse of a traditional kimchi under 10 minutes.

Servings: 2

Total Time: 10 minutes

Ingredients:

- 1 cup diced cabbage
- 1/2 cup vinegar
- 2 teaspoon red chili powder
- 1 inch ginger, diced
- Black pepper to taste
- 1/4 cup green onion, diced
- 8 cloves garlic, minced
- 2 tablespoon of virgin olive oil
- 2 teaspoon soy sauce
- 1 1/2 teaspoon of powdered sugar
- Salt to taste

Instructions:

In a mixing bowl combine the cabbage with green onions.

Add salt and crush the vegetables finely. Let it sit for 10 minutes.

In another bowl combine the ginger, garlic, soy sauce, sugar, black pepper, olive oil, vinegar and red chili powder.

Mix well and refrigerate until served.

Red Cabbage Kimchi

This kimchi recipe is a spin on the traditional Napa Cabbage kimchi. It is done with red cabbage and I have added bok choy to make it more interesting. It can be eaten with toast or can be added to fried rice or even burgers.

Servings: 1 jar

Total Time: 48 hours

Ingredients:

- 1 lb. red cabbage, chopped
- 1/3 cup kosher salt
- 1lb baby bok choy, diced
- 1/4 cup brown sugar
- 2 teaspoons garlic, grated
- 1 teaspoon ginger, grated
- 1 tsp red pepper flakes
- 2 tablespoons fish sauce
- 1 tablespoon toasted sesame oil
- Toasted sesame seeds

Instructions:

In a bowl combine the cabbage with the kosher salt. Mix in a way that the cabbage releases its juice.

Let it sit for 10 minutes. Wash the cabbage finely and rinse off.

Add it to a mason jar.

Add the remaining ingredients.

Mix well and cover with lid.

Let it sit for 48 hours.

Kale Chickpea Kimchi Salad

Have you ever tried kimchi salad before? If you haven't, try this recipe with chickpeas. It will blow your mind.

Servings: 4

Total Time: 1 hour

Ingredients:

- 1 cup chickpeas, soaked overnight
- 5 cups kale, chopped
- 1 avocado, diced
- 2 tbsp lemon juice
- ¼ tsp sea salt
- ½ cup kimchi
- Pepper to taste
- 1 tbsp olive oil
- 1 tsp red chili flakes
- 1 tsp soy sauce

Instructions:

Boil the chickpeas in salted water for 40 minutes.

Drain well and set aside for now.

In a mixing bowl, combine the chickpeas, kale, soy sauce, lemon juice, olive oil, kimchi, salt, pepper, and avocado and mix well. Serve fresh.

Asian Pears Kimchi

Pear has a very sweet and crunchy texture. It tastes really well when you make it into a kimchi.

Servings: 1 jar

Total Time: 48 hours

Ingredients:

- 2 Asian Pears
- 1/4 cup kosher salt
- 1/4 cup sugar
- 1/3 cup chives, diced
- 1/4 cup Korean red chile flakes
- 2 1/2 tablespoons fish sauce
- 1 inch ginger, grated
- 2 cloves garlic, grated
- 3 to 4 tablespoons water
- Black sesame seeds

Instructions:

Peel the pears and discard the cord.

Cut into semi thick slices.

Boil the pears in water for 10 minutes.

Drain and rinse well.

In a mixing bowl add everything together.

Put it in the jar and cover with lid. Let it ferment for nearly 48 hours.

Serve cold.

Mushroom Kimchi Fried Rice

Chinese fried rice gets Korean twist when you add kimchi to it. It enhances the flavor by 10 percent.

Servings: 4

Total Time: 1 hour

Ingredients:

- 1 cup brown mushroom, sliced
- 1 1/2 teaspoons sesame oil
- 2 eggs, beaten
- 1 cup green onion, diced
- 4 minced garlic cloves
- 3/4 cup kimchi
- 2 cup cooked brown rice
- 1 cup diced fresh spinach
- 1/2 cup green peas
- 1/4 cup kimchi juice
- 2 tablespoons soy sauce

Instructions:

In a large wok heat the oil.

Fry the egg until scrambled. Transfer to a plate.

In the same wok, fry the ginger, garlic, green onion for 1 minute.

Add the mushroom, and green peas, spinach, and toss for 3 minutes.

Add the soy sauce, kimchi juice, kimchi and toss for 5 minutes.

Finally add the cooked rice and toss for 3 minutes.

Serve hot.

Garlic Chives Kimchi

Garlic and chives really complement each other well. This kimchi is suitable with any type of dish you are eating. It goes well in any salad too.

Servings: 1 jar

Total Time: 36 hours

Ingredients:

- 1 lb. garlic
- 1 tablespoon rice powder
- ½ lb. chives
- 3 tablespoons red chili pepper flakes
- 1 teaspoon sesame seeds
- 1 tsp salt
- 3 tablespoons fish sauce
- 1 teaspoon sugar

Instructions:

Peel the garlic and cut them lengthwise.

Cut the chives into long strips.

Combine the salt, sesame seeds, red chili flakes, fish sauce and sugar in a bowl.

Mix the garlic and chives with the sugar mix.

Put it in a mason jar and cover with lid.

Let it ferment for 36 hours.

Serve cold.

Kimchi Tofu Chicken Soup

During the winter time, the Koreans love their kimchi soups. They add any type of meat in this traditional soup recipe. I have used chicken here.

Servings: 3-4

Total Time: 25 minutes

Ingredients:

- 1 cup diced tofu
- ½ cup kimchi
- 1 cup bulgogi mushrooms
- 1 cup chicken, boneless
- 1 tbsp soy sauce
- 1 tsp lime juice
- 3 cup chicken stock
- Salt and pepper to taste

Instructions:

In a pot add the chicken stock with chicken.

Cover with the lid. Cook the chicken for 10 minutes.

Add the kimchi, tofu, soy sauce, lime juice and mushrooms.

Cover and cook for about 15 minutes.

Serve hot.

Squash Kale Cabbage Kimchi Salad

Squash During the winter time, the Koreans love their kimchi soups. They add any type of meat in this traditional soup recipe. I have used chicken here.

Servings: 1-2

Total Time: 10 minutes

Ingredients:

- 1 cup diced squash
- ½ cup cabbage kimchi
- ¼ cup kale kimchi

Instructions:

Boil the squash in salted water for 5 minutes.

Drain well and rinse off the excess water.

In a mixing bowl add the diced squash.

Add the kale kimchi and the cabbage kimchi.

Mix well and serve fresh.

Scallion Apple Kimchi

Apple kimchi taste really great with bread or on toasts. It can also be eaten with tortilla and sometimes with rice. Adding scallion to this kimchi adds more flavors.

Servings: 1 jar

Total Time: 48 hours

Ingredients:

- Salt and pepper to taste
- 1 cup diced scallions
- 1 tsp soy sauce
- 4 tbsp vinegar
- 1 tbsp chili paste
- 1 tsp lime juice
- 2 green apples
- ½ cup brown sugar

Instructions:

Peel the apples and get rid of the cord. Cut them into small pieces.

Combine the apple and the scallion. Add salt and pepper to it.

Crush them well using your hands. Let it stand for 20 minutes.

Now add the vinegar, chili paste, brown sugar, lime juice, soy sauce and mix well.

Put the mix into a mason jar. Cover it tightly and let it ferment for 48 hours.

Pineapple Kimchi

Pineapple is a tropical fruit that cannot be found all through the year. To preserve pineapple, making kimchi is a good idea. It has a very tangy, and sweet flavors with a hint of spice in it.

Servings: 1 jar

Total Time: 36 hours

Ingredients:

- 1 cup pineapple cubes
- ½ cup brown sugar
- 1 tbsp lime juice
- 1 tbsp vinegar
- Salt to taste
- 1 tbsp paprika
- 1 tsp chili flakes

Instructions:

Combine the chili flakes, paprika, vinegar, salt, lime juice and brown sugar together.

Mix well and add pineapple to it.

Put the mix into a mason jar. Add the lid tightly.

Let it ferment for 36 hours. Preserve in a refrigerator.

Stuffed Onion Kimchi

Onion kimchi tastes good but when you stuff it and then make kimchi, it becomes an irresistible thing to eat. People relish stuffed onion kimchi by itself as it tastes so good.

Servings: 2 jars

Total Time: 72 hours

Ingredients:

- 6-8 large white onions
- 1 cup vinegar
- 1 cup fish sauce
- ½ cup brown sugar
- 1 tbsp olive oil
- Salt and pepper to taste
- ½ cup grated carrots
- ½ cup chopped spring onion
- ½ cup chili paste
- 1 tbsp grated garlic
- 1 tbsp grated ginger

Instructions:

Peel the onions and cut them in a way that the front becomes a pocket to stuff things in it.

Rub some salt to the onions and let it sit for 1 hour. Wash off the salt and rinse off.

Combine the remaining ingredients together.

Stuff the onions using the mixture.

Put them in mason jars. Cover tightly and let them ferment for 72 hours.

Stuffed Jalapeno Pepper Kimchi

Have you ever tried jalapeno pepper kimchi before? They taste even better when you stuff them. This recipe may seem like complicated but it is quite simple to make.

Servings: 2 jar

Total Time: 72 hours

Ingredients:

- 6-8 large jalapeno pepper
- 1 cup vinegar
- 1 tbsp sesame seeds
- 1 cup fish sauce
- ½ cup brown sugar
- Salt to taste
- ½ cup sliced carrots
- 2 tbsp sesame oil
- ½ cup chopped kale
- ½ cup chili paste
- 1 tbsp grated garlic
- 1 tbsp grated ginger

Instructions:

Combine the fish sauce, brown sugar, chili paste, sesame seeds, oil and salt together.

Add the sliced carrots, kale to the mix. Let it sit for 2 hours.

Cut one slit onto the jalapeno peppers so you can stuff them using the carrot mix.

Add the stuffing generously and rub the liquid onto the skin of the jalapeno peppers.

Let it ferment in an airtight container for 72 hours.

Carrot Kimchi

Carrot is a very beneficial vegetable for our health. Adding it in our everyday men it a great idea as it promotes good digestion, eye sight and it is good for our skin as well. Carrot kimchi is a good way to incorporate carrots in our breakfast, lunch and dinner.

Servings: 1 jar

Total Time: 48 hours

Ingredients:

- 1 cup sliced carrots
- ¼ cup chopped kale
- Salt to taste
- Black pepper to taste
- 1 tbsp chili paste
- 1 tbsp sesame seeds
- 1 tbsp paprika
- 1 tsp olive oil
- 1 tbsp vinegar
- 2 tbsp brown sugar
- 4 tbsp fish sauce

Instructions:

Combine the fish sauce, brown sugar, vinegar, oil, paprika, sesame seeds, chili paste, and pepper in a bowl.

Rub the salt to the carrots and kale. Let it stand for 30 minutes.

Wash the salt off and rinse off the vegetables.

Combine the vegetables with the chili paste mix.

Put the mix into a mason jar.

Cover with lid tightly and let it stand for fermenting for 48 hours.

Spring Onion Kimchi

This is a very simple spring onion kimchi that takes very little preparation. It can be added as a side dish to any dish.

Servings: 1 jar

Total Time: 36 hours

Ingredients:

- 1 cup spring onion
- 1 tbsp sesame seeds
- 2 tbsp sesame oil
- 2 tbsp brown sugar
- Salt to taste
- 2 tsp chili paste
- 1 tsp paprika
- 3 tbsp fish sauce
- 1 tbsp soy sauce

Instructions:

Combine the brown sugar, chili paste, paprika, soy sauce, fish sauce, sesame oil and mix well.

Cut off the stem of the spring onion. Wash them finely.

Rub salt to the spring onion generously. Put it aside for 60 minutes.

Wash the salt well and rinse off the spring onions.

Add the fish sauce mix and coat well.

Add the mix to a mason jar. Cover and let it ferment for 36 hours.

Pineapple Mango Cucumber Kimchi

There is nothing more appealing than a fruity kimchi. It can be paired with absolutely anything. It can be eaten by itself too.

Servings: 2 jars

Total Time: 36 hours

Ingredients:

- 1 cup cubed pineapples
- 1 cup cubed mangoes
- 1 cup sliced cucumber
- 1 scallion, chopped finely
- Salt to taste
- 3 tbsp chili paste
- 2 tbsp soy sauce
- 1 tbsp lime juice
- 2 tbsp vinegar
- 2 tbsp coconut oil

Instructions:

Combine the fruits and vegetables in a bowl. Add salt and coat well. Let it sit for 30 minutes.

Add the lime juice, soy sauce, coconut oil, vinegar, chili paste and mix well.

Let it ferment for 36 hours.

Refrigerate until served.

Mango Kimchi

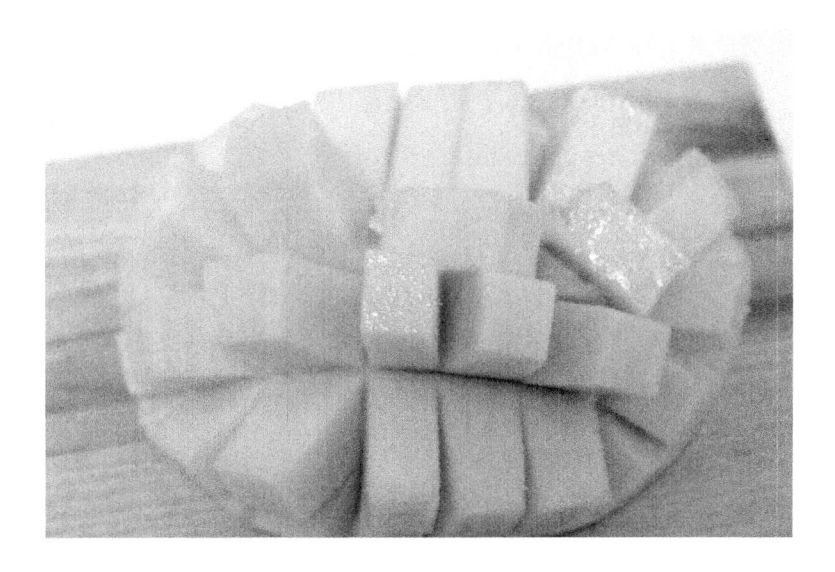

Mangoes are great as it is but when you make a kimchi out of it, it will blow your mind. This is a different take on the traditional kimchi recipes.

Servings: 1 jar

Total Time: 24 hours

Ingredients:

- 1 cup mango
- 4 tbsp chopped spring onion
- Salt to taste
- Black pepper to taste
- 1 tbsp chili paste
- 1 tsp vinegar
- 1 tsp soy sauce

Instructions:

Combine all the spices and sauces in a bowl.

Add the mango cubes. Toss well.

Add to a mason jar. Cover with lid and let it ferment for 24 hours.

Stuffed Cucumber Kimchi

Cucumber tastes really good when it is made into a kimchi. Stuffing it makes it unforgettable.

Servings: 2

Total Time: 72 hours

Ingredients:

- 4 large cucumbers
- 1 cup fish sauce
- ½ cup brown sugar
- Salt to taste
- ½ cup chopped chives
- 1 tbsp grated garlic
- 1 cup vinegar
- ½ cup chopped scallions
- ½ cup chili paste
- 1 tsp lime juice
- 1 tbsp grated ginger

Instructions:

Combine all the ingredients in a bowl except the cucumbers.

Cut the stem off the cucumbers. Cut them in a way that they become pockets to stuff things in it.

Add the stuffing inside and rub the rest of the mixture on the skin of the cucumber.

Add them to an airtight jar.

Let them ferment for 72 hours.

Broccoli Tempeh Kimchi Fried Rice

Frice rice is a Chinese traditional recipe and adding kimchi makes it slightly Korean. I have added Tempeh to it which makes it even more flavorful. Add your favorite type of veggies to make it more textureful.

Servings: 2

Total Time: 25 minutes

Ingredients:

- ½ cup cubed tempeh
- ½ cup diced broccoli
- 1 onion, diced
- 1 green chili, diced
- ½ cup kimchi
- 2 tbsp olive oil
- 1 cup rice
- 1 tbsp chopped spring onion
- ½ cup vegetable stock

Instructions:

Boil the rice in salted water until it is cooked.

Drain well and set the rice aside for now.

In a wok heat the oil.

Fry the onion, tempeh for 5 minutes.

Add the broccoli, and the vegetable stock. Cook for 5 minutes.

Add the rice, kimchi, spring onion, green chili and cook for about 5 minutes.

Serve hot.

Kale Kimchi

Kale kimchi may sound nothing interesting but it tastes very good with meat, in sandwiches and in stir fries. It contains a lot of health value too.

Servings: 1 jar

Total Time: 36 hours

Ingredients:

- 1 cup kale, chopped
- 2 tbsp chili paste
- 1 tbsp soy sauce
- 1 tsp chili flakes
- 1 tsp sesame seeds
- 2 tbsp fish sauce
- 2 tbsp brown sugar
- 2 tbsp vinegar
- Salt to taste

Instructions:

Wash the kale finely and rub them with salt generously.

Let it sit for 30 minutes. Wash off the salt with water and rinse well.

Combine the brown sugar, chili paste, chili flakes, sesame seeds, fish sauce, soy sauce and mix well.

Add the mix to the kale and mix well.

Put it in the mason jar and let it ferment for 36 hours.

Cabbage Radish Pear Kimchi

The traditional kimchi is made with cabbage, but when you want to make things interesting, you can add fruits like pear. I have gone one step further and added radish to it.

Servings: 2 jar

Total Time: 72 hours

Ingredients:

- 1 cup thinly sliced cabbage
- 1 cup thinly sliced radish
- ½ cup grated pear
- 2 tbsp chopped spring onion
- Salt to taste
- Pepper to taste
- ½ cup chili powder
- 1 cup vinegar
- ½ cup fish sauce
- 2 tbsp soy sauce
- 1 cup brown sugar

Instructions:

In a bowl combine the brown sugar, soy sauce, fish sauce, vinegar, salt, pepper and chili powder.

Rub salt generously to the fruits and veggies.

Let it sit for 1 hour. Wash off the excess salt.

Combine them with the chili mixture.

Put them in mason jars.

Let them ferment for 72 hours.

Broccoli Kimchi

Broccoli is the mother of all green vegetables. It is so beneficial for our health that many nutritionists tell us to add it to our everyday menu. Many people do not enjoy eating broccoli. They can try the taste of broccoli kimchi. It becomes very irresistible when made into a spicy and tangy kimchi.

Servings: 1 jar

Total Time: 48 hours

Ingredients:

- 1 cup diced broccoli florets
- ¼ cup sliced carrots
- ½ cup vinegar
- ½ cup fish sauce
- 2 tbsp chili paste
- Salt to taste
- 1 tbsp black pepper
- 1/3 cup brown sugar

Instructions:

Rub salt to the broccoli and carrots generously.

Let it sit for 40 minutes. Wash off the extra salt and rinse well.

Add the rest of the ingredients. Mix well.

Add to mason jar and add the lid tightly.

Let it ferment for 48 hours.

Spicy Cucumber Onion Kimchi Salad

Cucumber and onion Kimchi salad is something one can relish without adding any other dish to it. People who enjoy spices, would love this salad.

Servings: 2

Total Time: 5 minutes

Ingredients:

- 1 cup sliced cucumber
- ½ cup sliced spring onion
- ¼ cup diced white onion
- 2 tbsp kimchi
- 1 tsp sesame seeds
- 1 tsp soy sauce

Instructions:

Combine all the ingredients in a mixing bowl. Toss everything together. Serve fresh.

Peach Kimchi

Fruit kimchi has a really earthy and sweet texture to it. It can be used in a sandwich, as a topping to any dish or even in salads.

Servings: 1 jar

Total Time: 36 hours

Ingredients:

- 1 cup chopped peaches
- ¼ cup chopped red onion
- 1 tbsp lime juice
- 2 tbsp vinegar
- 4 tbsp brown sugar
- 1 tsp chili paste
- 1 green chili, chopped
- Salt to taste
- Black pepper to taste

Instructions:

Combine all the ingredients in a bowl.

Mix well and put it in a mason jar.

Add the lid tightly. Let it ferment for 36 hours.

Chicken Cabbage Kimchi Stir Fry

Chinese cuisine is famous for its stir fries. When you add kimchi to it, it gets a Korean twist. Try the recipe and it will blow your mind.

Servings: 2

Total Time: 20 minutes

Ingredients:

- 1 cup sliced chicken, boneless, skinless
- 1 tsp sesame seeds
- 2 tbsp olive oil
- ½ cup diced white onion
- ½ cup shredded cabbage
- ½ cup kimchi
- Salt and pepper to taste
- 1 tsp tomato paste

Instructions:

In a large wok heat the oil.

Add the onion and toss for 2 minutes.

Add the chicken and toss for 2 minutes.

Add the kimchi, tomato paste, salt, pepper, cabbage and toss for 8 minutes.

Add the sesame seeds and toss for another 5 minutes.

Serve hot.

Kimchi Noodles

If you try kimchi noodles once, you will not be able to eat regular noodles anymore. Kimchi add that special flavor to noodles that the flavor becomes unforgettable.

Servings: 2

Total Time: 20 minutes

Ingredients:

- 1 lb. ramen noodles
- 1 tsp sesame seeds
- 1/3 cup parmesan cheese
- Salt to taste
- White pepper to taste
- 1 tbsp tomato sauce
- ½ cup kimchi
- 1 tbsp chopped spring onion
- 1 egg yolk
- ½ cup sour cream
- 1 tbsp olive oil

Instructions:

Boil the ramen noodles in salted water.

In a wok heat the olive oil.

Add the sour cream, tomato sauce, salt, pepper and kimchi.

Toss for 5 minutes and add the boiled ramen.

Add the egg yolk, sesame seeds, parmesan cheese and cover with lid.

Cook for 2 minutes on low heat. Add the spring onion on top and serve hot.

Watermelon Rind Kimchi

Have you ever heard of using watermelon rind in anything? It is a common practice in many Asian countries. People who endorse zero wastage food tend to invent new food ideas and surprisingly it works quite well.

Servings: 2 jar

Total Time: 72 hours

Ingredients:

- 1 cup sliced watermelon rind
- 4 tbsp chili paste
- 4 tbsp fish sauce
- 2 tbsp soy sauce
- ½ cup brown sugar
- 1 tbsp minced garlic
- 1 tsp chili flakes
- 1 tbsp minced ginger
- Salt to taste
- ½ cup vinegar

Instructions:

Run the salt to the watermelon rind. Let it sit for 1 hour.

Wash the salt properly and rinse off well.

Add the rest of the ingredients.

Add to mason jars and cover the top tightly.

Let it ferment for 72 hours.

Conclusion

Eating healthy and well does not take much effort. You just need to be determined about doing a little extra to eat healthy and properly. All the kimchi recipes in the book are very simple to do. Anyone who has heard of kimchi for the first time can try making these kimchis too. The equipment required are easily found in your ordinary kitchen.

Try making these kimchis today and see how drastically your life changes.

Author's Afterthoughts

THANK YOU

Thanks ever so much to each of my cherished readers for investing the time to read this book!

I know you could have picked from many other books, but you chose this one. So, a big thanks for downloading this book and reading all the way to the end.

If you enjoyed this book or received value from it, I'd like to ask you for a favor. Please take a few minutes to post an honest and heartfelt review on Amazon.com. Your support does make a difference and helps to benefit other people.

Thanks for your Reviews!

Rachael Rayner

About the Author

Rachael Rayner

Are you tired of cooking the same types of dishes over and over again? As a mother of not one, but two sets of twins, preparing meals became very challenging, very early on. Not only was it difficult to get enough time in the kitchen to prepare anything other than fried eggs, but I was constantly trying to please 4 little hungry mouths under 5 years old. Of course I would not trade my angels for anything in the world, but I had just about given up on cooking, when I had a genius idea one afternoon while I was napping beside one of my sons. I am so happy and proud to tell you that since then, my kitchen has become my sanctuary and my children have become my helpers. I have transformed my meal preparation, my grocery shopping habits, and my cooking style. I am Racheal Rayner, and I am proud to tell you that I am no longer the boring mom sous-chef people avoid. I am the house in our neighborhood where every kid (and parent) wants to come for dinner.

I was raised Jewish in a very traditional household, and I was not allowed in the kitchen that much. My mother cooked the same recipes day in day out, and salt and pepper were probably the extent of the seasonings we were able to detect in the dishes she made. We did not even know any better until we moved out of the house. My husband, Frank is a foodie. I thought I was too, until I met him. I mean I love food, but who doesn't right? He revolutionized my knowledge about cooking. He used to take over in the kitchen, because after all, we were a modern couple and both of us worked full time jobs. He prepared chilies, soups, chicken casseroles—one more delicious than the last. When I got pregnant with my first set of twins and had to stay home on bed rest, I took over the kitchen and it was a disaster. I tried so hard to find the right ingredients and recipes to make the dishes taste something close to my husband's. However, I hated follow recipes. You don't tell a pregnant woman that her food tastes bad, so Frank and I reluctantly ate the dishes I prepared on week days. Fortunately, he was the weekend chef.

After the birth of my first set of twins, I was too busy to even attempt to cook. Sure, I prepared thousands of bottles of milk and purees, but Frank and I ended up eating take out 4 days out of 5. Then, no break for this mom, I gave birth to my second set of twins only 19 months later! I knew that now it was not just about Frank and I anymore, but it was about these little ones for whom I wanted to cook healthy meals, and I had to learn how to cook.

One afternoon in March, when I got up from that power nap with my boys, I had figured out what I needed to do to improve my cooking skills and stop torturing my family with my bland dishes. I had to let go of everything I had learned, tasted, or seen from my childhood and start over. I spent a week organizing my kitchen, and I equipped myself a new blender. I also got some fun shaped cookie cutters, a rolling pin, wooden spatulas, mixing bowls, fruit cutters, and plenty of plastic storage containers. I was ready.

My oldest twins, Isabella and Sophia are now teenagers, and love to cook with their Mom when they are not too busy talking on the phone. My youngest twins Erick and John, are now 10 years old and so helpful in the kitchen, especially when it's time to make cookies.

Let me start sharing my tips, recipes, and shopping suggestions with you ladies and gentlemen. I did not reinvent the wheel here but I did make my kitchen my own, started storing my favorite baking ingredients, and visiting the fresh produce market more often. I have mastered the principles of slow cooking and chopping veggies ahead of time. I have even embraced the involvement of my little ones in the kitchen with me.

I never want to hear you say that you are too busy to cook some delicious and healthy dishes, because BUSY, is my middle name.

Printed in Great Britain
by Amazon